\>\>\>\>\>\>\>   \>\>\> \>\>\>   \>\>\>\>\>\>\>

THE GOSPEL OF JUDAS

The Sarcastic Gospel

>>>>>>>   >>> >>>   >>>>>>>

THE GOSPEL OF JUDAS

The Sarcastic Gospel

by Mark M. Mattison

First Edition

© 2014 Mark M. Mattison. All rights reserved.

Scripture quotations marked DFV are from the *Divine Feminine Version* (DFV) of the New Testament, made publicly available through the Creative Commons License – Attribution, Noncommercial, Share Alike 3.0 United States. For full details see:
http://creativecommons.org/licenses/by-nc-sa/3.0/us

Scripture quotations marked NRSV are from the New Revised Standard Version Bible, Copyright © 1989 by the Division of Christian Education of the National Council of the Churches in Christ in the United States of America.

The Gospel of Judas: The Sarcastic Gospel

Contents

Acknowledgements	6
Introduction	7
1: Who Was Judas Iscariot?	10
2: Irenaeus on the Gospel of Judas	12
3: Judas Iscariot: Hero or Villain?	15
4: Judas' Gospel on Apostolic Christianity	20
5: Judas' Gospel on the Spiritual World	25
6: The Gospel of Judas	30
7: The Question of "Gnosticism"	40
8: The "Canon" of Scripture	45
Appendix: A Public Domain Version of the Gospel of Judas	49
Notes	62
Bibliography	70

Acknowledgements

I'd like to express my gratitude to all the women and men of the Grand Rapids Writer's Exchange who have played such an important role in my journey as a writer over the last seven years. Their constructive criticism of my writing has been invaluable.

Thanks are also due to those writers and readers who commented on the entire manuscript: Michelle Griswold, Isabella Riley, Rhonda Hoffman, Esther Yff-Prins, and Kathleen Gibbons. I'm particularly indebted to the extensive comments and constructive criticism of Lance Jenott, author of *The Gospel of Judas: Coptic Text, Translation, and Historical Interpretation of the 'Betrayer's Gospel.'* Dr. Jenott has kindly corrected several of my errors and offered many helpful suggestions; this book has been considerably improved as a result. Of course, I remain solely responsible for any errors or mistakes.

Finally, I'm deeply grateful to my wife, Rebecca, whose graceful and patient encouragement is a source of inexhaustible spiritual strength.

The Gospel of Judas: The Sarcastic Gospel

Introduction

In 2006, yet another sensational archaeological find stormed international media outlets. In April of that year, the National Geographic Society unveiled a restored copy of the fabled Gospel of Judas, long believed to have been completely lost to history. A few days later National Geographic aired a documentary about the find, which was followed by a flurry of books and articles debating its meaning and significance. Though few thought it might be a forgery, by 2013 scientific testing of the ink confirmed a date no later than the fourth century.[1] This fourth-century copy is a translation of a second-century Greek text, as we'll see in Chapter Two.

To gauge the meaning and significance of all this, it's important to consider this latest news in its broader historical context. It's well known that the twenty-seven books of the New Testament aren't the only books that early Christians wrote in the decades following Jesus' ministry.[2] Scores of other books, including other Gospels, preserved oral traditions and repackaged earlier Gospel narratives in new ways to address rapidly changing social and cultural challenges that early Christians faced. In the end, however, only four Gospels were permanently preserved in the church's official "canon" (standard) of official books representing "orthodox" Christianity, as we'll see in Chapter Eight. Most of the others were eventually lost to history.

Over the last century, however, many exciting archaeological discoveries have tremendously enhanced our understanding of early Christian history. In 1896 a German scholar brought a copy of the Gospel of Mary from Cairo, although it wasn't published until 1955.[3] Next came the

The Gospel of Judas: The Sarcastic Gospel

discovery of a dozen leather-bound codices (books) near Nag Hammadi in Egypt in 1945, which provided dozens of previously unknown early texts. This library contained several new Gospels, including the Gospel of Truth, the Gospel of Philip, and most famously the Gospel of Thomas, among others. Two years later the Dead Sea Scrolls were discovered, providing a treasure trove of early Jewish writings.

A few decades later, sometime in the 1970s, the codex containing the Gospel of Judas was discovered in Egypt, although it languished in obscurity in the antiquities market for decades before it was responsibly restored, translated, and finally published in 2006. Like the codex containing the Gospel of Mary and the codices containing the Nag Hammadi library, the codex containing the Gospel of Judas is written in Coptic, the ancient Egyptian language written in Greek letters. Coptic was commonly used from about 300 to 1000 CE.[4]

So we have yet another early Gospel to help us understand the growth and development of early Christianity. But what, precisely, does this Gospel have to offer? What is its true significance? That's where we find the controversy. And as with most controversies, many public arguments seem to generate more heat than light.

Fortunately, before digging into that controversy, we can easily answer the questions most people will have about this most unusual of Gospels. About these facts there is no debate. To begin with – no, the Gospel of Judas was not really written by Judas Iscariot. For that matter, it doesn't even claim to have been written by Judas. It wasn't even written by anybody who actually knew Judas, or during Judas' short lifetime, or within the first hundred years of when Judas lived.

This leads to the next obvious question: does the Gospel of Judas tell us anything new about Jesus, or about Judas, or about what really happened during Jesus' lifetime? Again, the answer has to be no. As we'll see, this Gospel tells us much more about what was happening in the fledgling church of the second century. In fact, as we'll see in Chapter Five, this appears to be its main significance.

Judas' Gospel may not offer additional spiritual insight like other noncanonical Gospels such as Mary or Thomas, but its historical significance is unmistakable as a testimony to what some early Christians believed. Put differently, what appears to be most important is what the anonymous author of Judas' Gospel has to say *about* Judas and the other disciples.

The most pronounced controversy hasn't been over what it might reveal about the first century, but over whether it reveals a completely unprecedented view of Judas in antiquity. Is the infamous Judas Iscariot really the protagonist of this Gospel? Is he portrayed as a hero instead of a villain? This question will be considered in Chapter Three.

In addition to commentary and reflections on Judas' Gospel, this book also contains a fresh new translation of the recovered text. Unlike most translations to date, however, this translation is more complete. Most previous translations, including those of National Geographic, Karen King, Willis Barnstone, and April DeConick, are based on the restored Coptic transcript prior to the recovery of the additional fragments published in 2010.[5] This translation incorporates the new fragments, providing a more complete version of Judas' Gospel.

In addition to the more colloquial translation provided in Chapter Six, this book also contains a more literal translation in the appendix which has been committed to the public domain. That version may be freely copied and used, in whole or in part, changed or unchanged, for any purpose.

The Gospel of Judas: The Sarcastic Gospel

1
Who Was Judas Iscariot?

Very little is said about Judas Iscariot in the New Testament, and nothing at all outside of the Gospels and the first chapter of Acts. He's remembered for one thing only: betraying Jesus to the authorities. Such little information about one of the most infamous scandals has fueled endless speculation ever since.

Matthew, Mark, Luke, and John all agree that Judas was an insider, one of the twelve disciples.[1] According to the first three Gospels, Judas had already conspired against Jesus with the temple authorities shortly before the Last Supper.[2] But why?

The earliest Gospel, Mark, doesn't disclose a specific motivation, but both Mark and Matthew describe Judas meeting with the authorities immediately following Jesus' anointing by a woman using very costly perfume.[3] Matthew's account more explicitly implies that Judas was motivated by money.[4] To this John's Gospel adds that Judas, the group's treasurer, was actually a thief (cf. John 12:6ff).

But there's more. According to the later canonical Gospels – Luke and John – something even more sinister was at work: "The devil had already given Judas Iscariot, Simon's son, the idea of betraying him" (cf. John 13:2, DFV). Both Luke and John write that "Satan" (literally, "Adversary" or "Enemy") actually "entered" Judas[5] to inspire him to go to the authorities.

All four canonical Gospels describe Jesus cryptically tipping his hand during his Last Supper, revealing his knowledge that one of his own was about to betray him.[6] John goes even further; since Jesus already knew "what was in" everyone (John 2:24,25 DFV), it was hard to imagine Jesus not knowing far in advance that one of his chosen twelve would turn out to be his betrayer. In John's Gospel, Jesus says early on, "'Haven't I chosen you Twelve? Yet one of you is a devil.' Jesus meant that one of the Twelve, Judas, son of Simon Iscariot, was going to betray him" (John 6:70,71, *The Inclusive Bible*).

Matthew and Luke, following Mark, dramatize the betrayal with the irony that Judas reveals Jesus' identity to the authorities by the prearranged signal of a friendly kiss.[7] After Jesus' arrest, trial, and execution, the last we hear of Judas involves his remorseful suicide[8] and replacement by another disciple (cf. Acts 1:16-26).

The New Testament Gospels, then, have nothing charitable to say about Judas, the traitor. He's a thief (at best) and inspired by Satan (at worst); in John's Gospel, Judas isn't just *inspired* by the devil (John 13:27), he *is* a devil (John 6:70).

Of course, Judas isn't the only disciple portrayed in a negative light; for example, Jesus famously calls Peter "Satan" for trying to stand in the way of his self-sacrifice[9] and announces to his twelve disciples that Satan intends "to sift all of you like wheat" (Luke 22:31, NRSV). Peter in particular, the disciple most vocal about his loyalty to Jesus,[10] is told he'll deny Jesus three times in a row.[11] But Judas is in a different category altogether; he doesn't simply desert or deny Jesus in these Gospels, he actually betrays him. It would have been better for him if he hadn't been born.[12]

In later Christian tradition, Judas fares even worse.[13] From the Gospels to Acts to medieval Christian tradition, Judas Iscariot is consistently and unilaterally portrayed as the villain of the Gospel story. That's been the consensus position – until now.

With the discovery of this new Gospel, have we finally discovered the one exception? Does Judas' Gospel actually portray Judas not as a greedy or evil turncoat, but as Jesus' closest confidant instead? Remarkably, an influential second-century bishop seemed to imply just that.

The Gospel of Judas: The Sarcastic Gospel

2
Irenaeus on the Gospel of Judas

As we saw in the Introduction, the Coptic codex containing the Gospel of Judas has been dated to the fourth century at the latest. This Coptic text in turn appears to be a translation of an earlier Greek text which has since been lost to history. But when was the original Gospel written? Could it have been written even earlier than the fourth century? As it turns out, yes – and we can confidently date it to the second century at the latest because of a specific reference to it in early Christian literature.

Prior to its rediscovery just a few decades ago, the Gospel of Judas was known only from a single source: a book written around 180 CE by a bishop of Lyons named Irenaeus. The first volume of his extensive work, *Against Heresies*, mentions people who supposedly revered Cain over Abel, Esau over Jacob, and other biblical characters on the wrong side of history. Later "Church Fathers" elaborated on this description, labeling these people "Cainites." Irenaeus describes them only briefly:

> They declare that Judas the traitor was thoroughly acquainted with these things, and that he alone, knowing the truth as no others did, accomplished the mystery of the betrayal; by him all things, both earthly and heavenly, were thus thrown into confusion. They produce a fictitious history of this kind, which they style the Gospel of Judas (*Adv. Haer.* I.31.1).

Clearly Irenaeus was describing exactly the same Gospel that the National Geographic Society unveiled in 2006. Though tantalizingly brief, this single statement at least confirms the

The Gospel of Judas: The Sarcastic Gospel

antiquity of Judas' Gospel; it couldn't have been written any later than Irenaeus' book, firmly situating it prior to 180 CE, probably sometime in the middle of the second century.

Irenaeus' description suggests that Judas was an enlightened protagonist in this Gospel; he knew "the truth as no others did" and "accomplished the mystery of the betrayal." And there does seem to be a certain logic to the idea. If Jesus really needed to die on the cross, might it not follow that Judas actually did him a favor by handing him over to the authorities? In his book *Judas and Jesus: Two Faces of a Single Revelation*, Jean-Yves Leloup describes it this way:

> In this history, Judas appears as an instrument of the divine plan. "But all this has taken place so that the scriptures of the prophets might be fulfilled," say the canonical gospels. Judas is a necessary actor for the revelation of the new Messiah – without him, there would have been no trial, no condemnation, no crucifixion, no resurrection, no Christianity.
>
> Hence, for the Cainite-Judaite community, to which the Gospel of Judas belongs, the man Judas was a major player in the drama of salvation. In the same spirit that the Roman liturgy celebrates the *felix culpa*, the "happy fault," of original sin "which brought us such a Redeemer," the Cainite-Judaite liturgy celebrated the "happy betrayal which brought us such a Savior."[1]

If Irenaeus was right, then the Gospel of Judas would be the only ancient text contradicting the New Testament's negative portrayal of Judas Iscariot; it would be an amazing anomaly. But now that we finally have direct access to this Gospel ourselves, some have questioned the accuracy of Irenaeus' representation.

According to Irenaeus, the Gospel of Judas was written by people who were later described as "Cainites." But if it was really a "Cainite" Gospel, why isn't Cain mentioned anywhere in it? In actual fact, it's not the name of Cain but rather the name of Cain's younger brother Seth who's mentioned in the text (p. 49). As will be seen in Chapter Seven below, this Gospel clearly belongs to a category of literature that reveres the biblical figure of Seth, so a tribute to Cain would seem out of place.

Is it possible that Irenaeus unintentionally misrepresented the people who wrote and read this Gospel? Perhaps he assumed that anyone who would revere Judas would also revere other villains throughout the biblical stories.[2] Irenaeus seems to have believed that the author of Judas' Gospel turned the biblical story on its head and turned Judas into a cosmic hero.

Based on what Judas' Gospel actually *says*, however, it appears that Irenaeus could have missed the whole point. His reaction would then be like that of someone reading a satire but not getting the joke. Unfortunately, his description is all that modern scholars had to go on before this Gospel actually turned up. When it was finally discovered, scholars fully expected to find the Gospel that Irenaeus described – the one Gospel that champions Judas as a hero instead of a villain.

The Gospel of Judas: The Sarcastic Gospel

3
Judas Iscariot: Hero or Villain?

In their book, *Reading Judas: The Gospel of Judas and the Shaping of Christianity,* renowned scholars Elaine Pagels and Karen L. King write:

> For thousands of years, Christians have pictured Judas as the incarnation of evil. Motivated by greed and inspired by Satan, he is the betrayer whom Dante placed in the lowest circle of hell. But the *Gospel of Judas* shows Judas instead as Jesus's closest and most trusted confidant – the one to whom Jesus reveals his deepest mysteries and whom he trusts to initiate the passion.[1]

This is by far the most controversial and explosive claim made by the National Geographic Society in April of 2006 when it announced the publication of the Gospel of Judas and aired its exclusive documentary: Judas is "the most gifted among [the disciples], the human hero of this 'gospel': Judas, the misunderstood – still its hero whatever his weaknesses."[2]

One of the members of the academic team assembled by the National Geographic Society, the prominent biblical scholar Bart D. Ehrman, writes at length about the negative portrayal of Judas throughout Christian history, adding:

> The Gospel of Judas provides an alternative vision. It is true that over the years some Christians have wondered if the consistent denigration of Judas was fair. Theologically, some have asked, if Christ had to die for the sins of the world, and Judas is the one that made it possible, wasn't that

The Gospel of Judas: The Sarcastic Gospel

a good thing? Something that Christ himself wanted? Moreover, some scholars have noted that with the passing of time our ancient traditions portray Judas in *increasingly* villainous ways. Could it be that in the very earliest traditions, which have now been lost, Judas was seen as an intimate of Jesus who simply did his master's will?

If Judas ever was portrayed this way, there is no surviving evidence of it, no text that speaks of Judas in any positive way – until now. The Gospel of Judas stands alone in insisting that Judas was not only close to Jesus but was also the only one among the disciples who understood who Jesus was and did what he wanted.[3]

Is that really what Judas' Gospel portrays – that Judas, the presumed villain and traitor of Jesus, was actually Jesus' closest and most trusted disciple? That Jesus actually wanted him to conspire with the authorities to arrange for his own arrest and crucifixion?

Just a year after the National Geographic's sensational media announcement, another prominent scholar, April DeConick, published a book challenging this interpretation of Judas' Gospel.[4] Her incisive arguments about the correct translation of key passages are compelling.

But why wouldn't this Gospel portray Judas as the protagonist? Isn't it, after all, "The Gospel of Judas"? That is the title given to this book in the Coptic codex. However, as Ehrman himself notes, there is a key difference between the title of this Gospel and the title of other Gospels. Other Gospels are typically titled "The Gospel According to" someone: "The Gospel According to Matthew," "The Gospel According to Mary," "The Gospel According to Thomas," and so on. But this Gospel's title is different; it isn't "The Gospel *According to* Judas," it's more ambiguously "The Gospel *of* Judas."[5] Though Judas is the main character in this text (besides Jesus) – in fact, the only disciple singled out by name and privy to extended revelations from Jesus – nevertheless this Gospel is avowedly

The Gospel of Judas: The Sarcastic Gospel

not "good news" for Judas. It is, rather, a Gospel story – a narrative about Jesus' mission and message – which features Judas as Jesus' principal dialogue partner. Not as a trusted friend or confidant, but rather as a tragic figure.

A couple of passages near the end of the Gospel are key. In one of them, on page 56, Jesus tells Judas that he'll "do more than all of" the other disciples. National Geographic's translation reads, "you will exceed all of them." King and Barnstone both use the word "surpass" instead of "exceed." But the Coptic term here means simply "more than";[6] it doesn't necessarily imply a positive or a negative connotation, so multiple interpretations are possible. Considering the context, DeConick translates this text differently: "You will do worse than all of them."[7]

Another key passage on page 57 describes Judas looking up to see a "luminous cloud," and goes on to say that "he entered it" and ascended to heaven. In the original Coptic transcript published by National Geographic, it was not clear who "he" was who entered the cloud. Was it Jesus or rather Judas? The footnote in *The Critical Edition* opines that the "he" in this text "is probably Judas,"[8] but in the article disclosing the new fragments, Marvin Meyer writes that the new fragment of page 58:

> clarifies who it is that enters the cloud with the sentence, following the voice from the cloud, "And Judas saw Jesus no more." As a number of our colleagues have offered, and it is in fact Jesus who enters the cloud near the end of the Gospel of Judas.[9]

Far from being the hero of this Gospel, Judas is actually described as a "demon" (p. 44) – no less a villain than in Luke or John (cp. John 6:70). In Judas' Gospel, Jesus does reveal everything to Judas, but not so that he can personally benefit from it; the corrected Coptic transcript is quite clear on that. He reveals "the mysteries of the kingdom" to Judas "Not so that

The Gospel of Judas: The Sarcastic Gospel

you'll go there, but you'll grieve much" (p. 35).[10] Judas also asks, "What good has it done me that you've separated me from that generation?" (p. 46).[11]

Finally, as Lance Jenott has pointed out, at the end Jesus tells Judas that "your anger has been kindled" (p. 56) and Judas subsequently hands Jesus over in exchange for money, just as in the canonical Gospels.[12] These are hardly the actions of a benevolent protagonist.

In other words, this isn't a story about the master passing along the keys of the kingdom to his successor; it's rather the kind of revelation that occurs in the final act of a drama or murder mystery in which the protagonist and the antagonist face off and reveal the rest of the plot before the final and tragic end of one of them. Jesus' revelation escalates the drama of the narrative and makes Judas' betrayal all the more tragic; he goes to his end in the full knowledge of what's going to happen to him and what he's going to be missing.

Yet if this interpretation is correct – if Judas' Gospel does *not* in fact portray a fundamentally different Judas, a hero instead of a villain – then how could the original team of highly competent scholars have gotten the story so wrong? Arguably there are a number of reasons – including the lasting influence of Irenaeus of Lyons. As DeConick notes, this goes a long way toward explaining why those who initially worked with the text got off on the wrong foot.[13]

Another reason DeConick cites is that the National Geographic's team of scholars was rushed; they found themselves translating and interpreting the text at the same time that they were working to restore it and piece all the fragments back together again.[14] In addition, they had been required to sign nondisclosure agreements as a precondition to working with the text, precluding the type of peer review and vetting that would have helped to ensure the accuracy of their findings.[15]

But perhaps the most significant reason for the initial misreading remains a broader concern about Christian anti-Semitism. This concern is articulated front-and-center in

The Gospel of Judas: The Sarcastic Gospel

National Geographic's 2006 documentary and repeated in the first books written about the recovered Gospel.[16]

Why should the story of Judas have any bearing on the issue of anti-Semitism? As scholars have long noted, the name "Judas" literally means "Jew." Ehrman writes: "In late Christian anti-Semitic rhetoric [Judas] becomes the proto-typical Jew: a greedy, money-grubbing, God-denying Christ-killer."[17] A Gospel portraying Judas as a hero rather than a villain, it was hoped, could likewise reverse centuries of Christian stereotypes.

However, even if Judas' Gospel did vindicate Judas Iscariot, that wouldn't necessarily undermine anti-Semitism. As King and Pagels note, Judas' Gospel still portrays Jews and Jewish priests in a negative light.[18] The significance of Judas' Gospel, then, is not that it provides a previously unknown and revolutionary understanding of Judas Iscariot or that it can somehow address the problem of Christian anti-Semitism. To find its real significance, we must look elsewhere.

The Gospel of Judas: The Sarcastic Gospel

4
Judas' Gospel on Apostolic Christianity

Appraising the real significance of Judas' Gospel, especially for contemporary readers, is no easy task. Unfortunately, some profound spiritual mystics who have commented so incisively on other noncanonical texts, including Cynthia Bourgeault and Jean-Yves Leloup, have barely commented on the contents of Judas' Gospel.

Bourgeault refers only briefly to it in her book *The Wisdom Jesus: Transforming Heart and Mind – a New Perspective on Christ and His Message*.[1] She makes only two assertions about this text, and both of them are wrong. First, she writes that it's part of the Nag Hammadi collection,[2] even though it wasn't found among the codices discovered near Nag Hammadi. Second, she writes that she "didn't blink an eye through all the public uproar" about a Gospel claiming that Judas wasn't really a traitor, since she had already been introduced to the idea that what Judas was really doing was leading the authorities on a wild goose chase to "buy time" for Jesus to complete the Last Supper.[3] However, as we've seen, that's not at all what Judas' Gospel portrays.

Similarly, in his book *Judas and Jesus: Two Faces of a Single Revelation*, Jean-Yves Leloup doesn't comment on the actual contents of Judas' Gospel. His entire discussion of the text is rather a reflection on the "Cainites" supposedly described by Irenaeus,[4] and he too assumes that Judas' Gospel portrays Judas as a protagonist, just as Irenaeus appears to say. The only other clue that may imply something about Leloup's understanding of Judas' Gospel is a footnote by the translator, Joseph Rowe, who describes Judas' Gospel as "Gnostic," an idea we'll discuss in Chapter Seven.

The Gospel of Judas: The Sarcastic Gospel

When we consider the actual contents of Judas' Gospel, what's probably most surprising isn't what we read about Judas, but rather what we read about Jesus' other disciples. No other disciple is named in the Gospel, but "the twelve disciples" are prominently featured as a group (pp. 33,44), and they're consistently portrayed as unspiritual. Jesus often laughs at his disciples (pp. 34,36,44,55), mocking their practice of communion (p. 34) and accusing them of all kinds of misdeeds, including shocking crimes like human sacrifice and murder (pp. 38,39). Jesus assures the twelve that they have no idea of who he really is (p. 34). Judas, the "demon" (p. 44), may not be a protagonist in this Gospel, but the other disciples aren't protagonists either; they're not even as perceptive as Judas, who at least understands who Jesus is. "I know who you are," Judas tells Jesus on page 35; "You've come from the immortal realm of Barbelo." (Though Judas' Gospel doesn't actually explain who "Barbelo" is, in related texts[5] "Barbelo" is described as the divine Mother.)

At any rate, *all* the disciples, including "the twelve," struggle against Jesus and lead astray the faithful. What are we to make of all this? Scholars agree that the second-century context of Judas' Gospel holds the answer. Many Christian leaders claimed that their authority came directly from Jesus' first disciples. Ehrman describes the argument:

> Christ appointed the apostles, the apostles appointed their own successors, their successors appointed the current bishops of the leading churches. Whatever these successors taught, therefore, came straight through a line of succession from Christ himself. ... since Jesus [in Judas' Gospel] seems to indicate that the apostles' followers will behave in a similar way, this text appears to be attacking not just the Twelve but the so-called apostolic successors. In the orthodox writings of the period, apostolic succession was used to guarantee the truth of the claims of the leaders of the Christian churches. Here it is used to show the

continued misunderstanding and incomprehensible behavior of those who claim the apostolic mantle for themselves. The leaders of the apostolic churches preach error and propagate immorality.[6]

Appeals to "apostolic" authority are apparent even in the pages of the New Testament books themselves. 1 John 1:2,3 emphasizes that those who knew Jesus "proclaim to you what we've seen and heard so that you also may partner with us" (1 John 1:3, DFV). Luke's Gospel counts among its sources "those who from the beginning were eyewitnesses" (Luke 1:2, DFV), and the Acts of the Apostles depicts a very orderly conferring of authority through "the twelve" to other apostolic leaders, including Paul, the apostle to the Gentiles.[7]

However, not all the Gospel authors were as positive in their portrayal of Jesus' disciples. In Mark's Gospel, Jesus' disciples constantly misunderstand Jesus. "According to the Gospel of Mark," DeConick writes, "the disciples are faithless and ignorant, failing to understand who Jesus is even though he has handpicked them as disciples."[8] As scholars have long noted, the characters in Mark's Gospel who fully recognize who Jesus is aren't the disciples, but rather Jesus' enemies, including the centurion who witnesses his death (Mark 15:39) and, most notably, the demons.[9] Similarly, in Judas' Gospel, none of Jesus' disciples recognize who Jesus is (p. 34) except for Judas (p. 35), the demon (p. 44).

Judas' Gospel, then, isn't entirely inconsistent with canonical Christian texts in its portrayal of Jesus' disciples. Most sources (e.g., Matthew, Luke, John, Acts) portray the disciples as Jesus' immediate successors and the guarantors of apostolic truth; others, including Galatians[10] and Mark's Gospel, are more ambivalent (at best) about Jesus' disciples.

In the second-century context of Judas' Gospel, arguments about the apostles were essentially arguments about church authority. Who had the authority to lead communities of the faithful on behalf of Christ? When bishops claimed to derive

The Gospel of Judas: The Sarcastic Gospel

their authority directly from Jesus' first disciples through a direct line of apostolic succession, were they to be trusted? The author of Judas' Gospel castigates the ministers who claimed to be the heirs of Jesus' first disciples. The vehicle this author uses to do that is a satirical Gospel in which the disciples represent second-century church leaders.

One of the key criticisms is that the disciples (and their successors) lead astray the faithful and even practice human sacrifice (pp. 38,39). This appears to reflect a debate about martyrdom in the early church. Pagels and King write:

> When we place the gospel in the context of what we know about Christians in the second century, the period when the *Gospel of Judas* was written, we can see [this author] as a Christian who takes a strong – and, ultimately, losing – stance on an issue that intensely engages Christians at his time: the continuing persecution of Jesus' followers at the hands of the Romans.[11]

For the author of Judas' Gospel, church leaders who preached the value of martyrdom were guilty of human sacrifice. Since these leaders traced their authority directly to Jesus' original disciples, the author of Judas' Gospel portrayed these disciples as themselves guilty of human sacrifice. Its condemnation of Jesus' disciples, then, is a thinly-veiled condemnation of second-century church leaders.[12]

On the other hand, some scholars have overemphasized this point, arguing that Judas' Gospel criticizes not only "orthodox" church leaders but other aspects of "orthodoxy" as well, including baptism, communion, and the significance of Jesus' death.[13] But Judas' Gospel does not explicitly challenge any of those things. Jesus criticizes the disciples' practice of communion, to be sure (p. 34) – and by extension the celebration of the Eucharist by self-avowed church authorities – but that need not imply that the author disapproved of communion entirely.[14] As we'll see in Chapter Seven, sometimes scholars overemphasize the differences between canonical Gospels and noncanonical Gospels.

Other examples can be cited in which Judas' Gospel isn't far removed from canonical scriptures. When Jesus says in Judas' Gospel that "no one born [of] this realm will see that (spiritual) generation ... and no person of mortal birth will be able to join it" (p. 37), how much different is that from texts like John 3:3, where Jesus says that "no one can see the kingdom of God without being born from above" (NRSV) or 1 Corinthians 15:50, where Paul writes that "flesh and blood cannot inherit the kingdom of God" (NRSV)?[15] And when Jesus appears to say that baptism in his name "will destroy the whole generation of the earthly Adam" (p. 56), how much different is that from texts like Romans 6:6, where Paul writes that "our old humanity" is "done away with" in baptism (DFV)?[16]

Like other early Christian texts, Judas' Gospel strongly affirms that this world is not all that there is; there exists a vast spiritual realm beyond the distractions of this physical creation, and the supposed authorities who dominate others do not really wield ultimate authority. In fact, their days are numbered; divine judgment awaits these illegitimate authorities.

Unlike the canonical Christian texts, however, Judas' Gospel provides an elaborate mythological description of the heavenly realm and the God who created the physical world.

The Gospel of Judas: The Sarcastic Gospel

5
Judas' Gospel on the Spiritual World

The epistles and Gospels of the canonical New Testament describe the physical and spiritual worlds in terms of multiple layers of reality. No single text provides a comprehensive "map" of the spiritual world, but brief descriptions scattered throughout imply a complex cosmological structure. In his descriptions of "visions and revelations," for example, Paul describes an ostensibly out-of-body experience, being caught up "into Paradise" located in "the third heaven" (2 Cor. 12:1-4, DFV).

At the other end of the spectrum, 1 Peter 3:19 describes a postmortem Jesus proclaiming his victory over "spirits in prison," spiritual beings described in 2 Peter 2:4 as disobedient "angels ... sent to Tartarus ... in chains of darkness to be kept for judgment" (2 Peter 2:4, DFV; cf. Jude 6). In Greek mythology, Tartarus was the prison of most of the mighty primordial Titans.

The spiritual world is described as populated with a variety of invisible spiritual beings, many of them malevolent, variously identified as "rulers," "authorities," "powers," "dominions," "angels," and so on.[1] Ephesians describes the spiritual life as a struggle against these cosmic forces:

> For our struggle is not against enemies of blood and flesh, but against the rulers, against the authorities, against the cosmic powers of this present darkness, against the spiritual forces of evil in the heavenly places (Eph. 6:12, NRSV).

The Gospel of Judas: The Sarcastic Gospel

These malevolent divine beings are ruled by a supreme evil spirit described as "the ruler of the power of the air, the spirit that is now at work among those who are disobedient" (Eph. 2:2, NRSV). In John 14:30, Jesus declares that "the ruler of this world is coming, and we have nothing in common" (DFV). Paul even goes so far as to describe this deceiving spirit as "the god of this world" (2 Cor. 4:4, DFV).

Judas' Gospel is not far removed from these canonical scriptures when it envisions a vast spiritual landscape populated by a hierarchy of divine beings, including a powerful malevolent spiritual being who rules over the created world order. Unlike the canonical epistles and Gospels, however, Judas' Gospel provides a more detailed description of this divine realm, starting on page 47 of the codex.

There, Jesus describes "a great and boundless realm whose horizons no angelic generation has seen." In this realm exists a great invisible Spirit, from whom emerged "the Self-Begotten, the God of light" (p. 47). The Self-Begotten in turn created four angels as attendants. Under them were created "myriads of angels without number to offer service" (p. 48). Twelve realms of twelve luminaries are described as "the father" of the "seventy-two luminaries," who "themselves made three hundred sixty luminaries appear in the incorruptible generation according to the Spirit's will so that there'd be five for each" (p. 49), completing a full 360 degrees (so to speak) of a supremely divine population.[2]

Underneath this incorruptible generation, however, Chaos and Hades are ruled by lower divine beings including "Nebro" ("Rebel") and "Saklas" ("Fool"). Together Nebro and Saklas created twelve angels who apparently produced another twelve (the text is difficult to follow at this point). The first five are identified as Yaoth,[3] Harmathoth, Galila, Yobel, and Adonaios. These in turn assisted Saklas in the creation of Adam and Eve:

The Gospel of Judas: The Sarcastic Gospel

> Then Saklas told his angels, 'Let's create a human being after the likeness and the image.' And they fashioned Adam and his wife Eve (p. 52).

This is the main theological point on which Judas' Gospel differs from what has become the canonical tradition. Not in its portrayal of Judas as a demonically-inspired betrayer; not in its portrayal of Jesus' disciples as ignorant and clueless, or in its valuation of communion and baptism; not even in its complex view of a highly-developed spiritual hierarchy, culminating in the creation of a malevolent ruling spirit who deceives the physical world. The most prominent difference is undoubtedly Judas' identification of this malicious divine spirit with the creator of the physical world.

The idea of the creator as an inferior divine being (known as the "demiurge" or "craftsman") was actually widespread in the ancient world. What suggests that the idea is ominous in this context is that this creator is identified with the malevolent Saklas, whom not only the disciples (p. 34) but also the twelve tribes of Israel (p. 55) are said to serve with blood sacrifices. In a Gentile Christian context, it's difficult to understand this characterization as anything short of anti-Jewish.

Its characterization of Judaism isn't the only harsh feature of Judas' Gospel, however. Another is its portrayal of homosexuality. On two pages, this Gospel criticizes presumably male church leaders who "sleep with men" (pp. 38,39, Public Domain Version). Like other early Christian writers, the author of Judas' Gospel doesn't recognize the biology of sexual orientation. Similarly, unlike some noncanonical Gospels (like Mary's Gospel), Judas' Gospel doesn't seem to have anything empowering or liberating to say about women or other minorities; apart from a fleeting reference to the mythological Barbelo on page 35 (who's surprisingly absent from the creation myth on page 47), the only women even mentioned in this Gospel are Eve (p. 52) and the wives of unfaithful church leaders (p. 38), and even then their only role is as passive marriage partners.[4]

This is what arguably makes Judas' Gospel most difficult for us to appreciate today. In the context of contemporary Christianity, this Gospel is an anti-Jewish, anti-social text, dripping with sarcasm and caustic in its attacks against its ideological opponents, the leaders of the developing institutional church.

Of course, Judas' Gospel is not unique in castigating others who are different; many other early Christian texts also criticize Jews, women, minorities, etc. But also like other early Christian texts, in spite of its negative rhetoric Judas' Gospel simultaneously points beyond itself to more profound spiritual realities.

First and foremost is the fact that there exists a vast spiritual dimension far beyond the limited physical world that we can perceive with our physical senses. In fact, this spiritual world is inaccessible to those who have not experienced a spiritual awakening.

Second, there's no good reason to unquestionably entrust our spiritual well-being to self-professed guarantors of ultimate truth who claim that they alone are authorized by tradition to speak and act in Jesus' name (pp. 38-40). Actions speak louder than words, and anyone who doesn't demonstrate spiritual insight in their personal conduct doesn't deserve to be followed by those who aspire to spiritual liberation.

Even Judas' tragic role in this story can be instructive; though Jesus reveals everything to Judas, the apostate disciple persists in his self-destructive journey. He's not unlike the "hearers of the word and not doers ... those who look at themselves in a mirror; for they look at themselves and, on going away, immediately forget what they were like" (Jas. 2:23,24, NRSV).

Though the Jesus of this Gospel laughs in derision at those who resist him, he also points to a better way, the possibility of a life beyond the meaningless and destructive patterns of selfish

The Gospel of Judas: The Sarcastic Gospel

living, an abundant and fulfilling life as part of "the great generation with no king" (p. 43).

Finally, Judas' Gospel demonstrates some of the breadth and depth of diversity among early followers of Jesus. It affords a rare glimpse into some of the heated controversies that engulfed second-century communities of Christians who struggled not only with the oppressive social forces around them but with each other as well, especially over the question of authority in the fledgling church. Over time, that question was largely settled in favor of bishops who grounded their authority in a doctrine of apostolic succession. But that authority never went unquestioned, as we can now see in the pages of this surprising recovered Gospel – the sarcastic Gospel of Judas.

The Gospel of Judas: The Sarcastic Gospel

6
The Gospel of Judas

The translation that follows is based on the Codex Tchacos, page 33 through page 58 (TC, *3*, 33 - 58). It's a fourth-century Coptic translation of an earlier Greek text dating to the middle of the second century (prior to 180 CE).

The text in Codex Tchacos, which remains our only known copy of this Gospel to date, is still missing several fragments. The fragments which became available after the publication of National Geographic's critical edition have been included in this translation, but many gaps in the manuscript remain. These gaps are indicated in the translation by brackets, and all words in brackets are proposed reconstructions. Words in parentheses are strictly editorial insertions to clarify the meaning of the text.

In addition to the more colloquial translation below, a more literal public domain translation has been included in the Appendix for further study.

Introduction

33 This is the secret message of judgment Jesus told Judas Iscariot over a period of eight days, three days before he celebrated Passover.

When he appeared on earth, he did signs and great wonders for the salvation of humanity. Some [followed] the way of justice, but others continued in their wrongdoing, so the twelve disciples were called. He started to tell them about the mysteries beyond the world and what would happen at the end. Often he didn't reveal himself to his disciples, but you'd find him in their midst as a child.

The Gospel of Judas: The Sarcastic Gospel

Jesus Criticizes The Disciples

One day he was with his disciples in Judea. He found them sitting together acting pious. When he [came up to] his disciples **34** sitting together praying over the bread, [he] laughed.

"Master," his disciples asked him, "why are you laughing at [our] prayer? What have we done? [This] is the right thing to do."

In response he told them, "I'm not laughing at you. You're not doing this because you want to, but because through this your God [will be] praised."

"Master," they said, "you […] are the Son of our God!"

Jesus asked them, "How do [you] know me? Truly [I] tell you, no generation of the people among you will know me."

When his disciples heard this, [they] started to get angry and furious and started to curse him in their hearts.

But when Jesus noticed their ignorance, [he asked] them, "Why are you letting your anger trouble you? Has your God within you and [his stars] **35** become angry with your souls? If any of you is [strong enough] among humans to bring out the perfect Humanity, stand up and face me."

All of them said, "We're strong enough." But their spirits weren't brave enough to stand before [him] – except Judas Iscariot. He was able to stand before him, but he couldn't look him in the eye, so he looked away.

"I know who you are," Judas [told] him, "and where you've come from. You've come from the immortal realm of Barbelo, and I'm not worthy to utter the name of the one who's sent you."

Then Jesus, knowing that he was thinking about what's exalted, told him, "Come away from the others and I'll tell you the mysteries of the kingdom. Not so that you'll go there, but you'll grieve much **36** because someone else will replace you to complete the twelve [elements] before their God."

"When will you tell me these things," Judas asked him, "and when will the great day of light dawn for the generation […]?"

But when he said these things, Jesus left him.

Another Generation

The next morning, he appeared to his disciples. "Master," they asked him, "where did [you] go? What did you do after you left us?"

Jesus told them, "I went to another great and holy generation."

"Lord," his disciples asked him, "what great generation is better and holier than us, that's not in these realms?"

Now when Jesus heard this, he laughed. "Why are you wondering in your hearts about the strong and holy generation?" he asked them. **37** "Truly I tell you, no one born [of] this realm will see that [generation], no army of angels from the stars will rule over it, and no person of mortal birth will be able to join it, because that generation doesn't come from [...] that has become [...] the generation of the people among [them] is from the generation of the great people [...] the powerful authorities who [...] nor the powers [...] those by which you rule."

When his disciples heard these things, they were all troubled in their spirits. They couldn't say a thing.

The Disciples' Vision

Another day Jesus came up to them.

"Master," they told him, "we've seen you in a dream, because we had great [dreams last] night."

"Why [...] hidden yourselves?" Jesus asked.

38 They [said, "We saw] a great [house, with a great] altar [in it, and] twelve people; we'd say they were priests. There was a name, and a crowd of people waiting at the altar [until] the priests [finished receiving] the offerings. We kept waiting too."

"What were they like?" [Jesus asked].

"[Some] fast [for] two weeks," they said. "Others sacrifice their own children; others their wives, praising and humbling themselves among each other. Others sleep around with men; others murder; yet others commit many sins and do criminal things. [And] the people standing [before] the altar invoke your [name]! **39** And in all their sacrificing, they fill the [altar] with their offerings." When they said this, [they] fell silent because they were troubled.

"Why are you troubled?" Jesus asked them. "Truly I tell you, all the priests standing before that altar invoke my name. [Again], I tell you, my name has been written on this [house] of the generations of the stars by the human generations. In my name [they] have shamefully planted fruitless trees." Jesus told them, "You're the ones receiving the offerings on the altar you've seen. That's the God you serve, and you're the twelve people you've seen. The animals you saw brought in to be sacrificed are the crowd you lead astray **40** before that altar. [Your minister] will stand up and use my name like that, and [the] generations of the pious will be loyal to him. After him, another person will present [those who sleep around], and another those who murder children, and another those who sleep around with men, and those who fast, and the rest of impurity, crime, and error. As for those who say, 'We're equal to the angels' – they're the stars that finish everything. The human generations have been told, 'Look, God has accepted your sacrifice from the hands of priests,' that is, the minister of error. But the Lord who commands is the Lord over everything. On the last day, they'll be found guilty.

41 "Stop [sacrificing animals]," Jesus told [them]. "You've [offered them] over the altar, over your stars with your angels where they've already been completed. So let them become [...] with you and let them [become] clear."

His disciples [said], "Cleanse us from our [sins] that we've committed through the deceit of the angels."

"It's not possible [...], nor [can] a fountain quench the fire of the entire inhabited world," Jesus told them. "Nor can a [city's] well satisfy all the generations, except the great, stable one. A single lamp won't illuminate all the realms, except the second generation, nor can one baker feed all creation **42** under [heaven].''

[When the disciples heard] these [things], they told [him], "Master, help and save us!"

"Stop struggling against me," Jesus told them. "Each one of you has your own star, [and ...] of the stars will [...] what belongs to it [...] I wasn't sent to the corruptible generation, but to the strong and incorruptible generation, because no enemy has ruled [over] that generation, nor any of the stars. Truly I tell you, the pillar of fire will fall quickly and that generation won't be moved by the stars."

Jesus and Judas

When Jesus [said] these things, he left, [taking] Judas Iscariot with him. He told him, "The water on the exalted mountain is [from] **43** [...] it didn't come to [water ... the well] of the tree of this realm's [fruit ...] after a time [...], but came to water God's paradise and the enduring [fruit], because [it] won't corrupt that generation's [way of life], but [it will exist] for all eternity."

Judas asked [him, "Tell] me, what kind of fruit does this generation have?"

"The souls of every human generation will die," Jesus said. "However, when these people have completed their time in this kingdom and their spirit leaves them, their bodies will die but their souls will live, and they'll be taken up."

"What will the rest of the human generations do?" Judas asked.

"It's not possible **44** to sow on [rock] and harvest its fruit," Jesus said. "In the same way, it's [not possible to sow on] the [defiled] race, the perishable wisdom, [and] the hand which created mortal humans so that their souls may go up to the realms above. [Truly] I tell you, [no ruler], angel, [or] power will be able to see the [places] that [this great], holy generation [will see]." When Jesus said this, he left.

The Gospel of Judas: The Sarcastic Gospel

"Master," Judas said, "just as you've listened to all of them, now listen to me too, because I've seen a great vision."

Jesus laughed when he heard this. "Why are you all worked up, you thirteenth demon?" he asked. "But speak up, and I'll bear with you."

"In the vision," Judas told him, "I saw myself. The twelve disciples were stoning me and **45** chasing [me rapidly]. Then I came to the place where [I had followed] you. I saw [a house there], but my eyes couldn't [measure] its size. Great people surrounded it, and that house had a roof of greenery. In the middle of the house was [a crowd …]. Master, take me in with these people!"

In response [Jesus] said, "Your star has led you astray, Judas." He continued, "No person of mortal birth is worthy to enter the house you've seen, because that place is reserved for those who are holy. Neither the sun nor the moon will rule there, nor the day, but those who are holy will always stand in the realm with the holy angels. Look, I've told you the mysteries of the kingdom **46** and I've taught you about the error of the stars and […] sent [on high] over the twelve realms."

"Master," Judas said, "Surely my progeny doesn't dominate the rulers, does it?"

In response Jesus told him, "Come, let me [tell] you [about the holy generation. Not so that you'll go there], but you'll be sorry when you see the kingdom and all its generation."

When Judas heard this, he asked him, "What good has it done me that you've separated me from that generation?"

In response Jesus said, "You'll become the thirteenth, and will be cursed by the other generations and will rule over them. In the last days they'll […] to you so you won't go up **47** to the holy generation."

Jesus Reveals Everything to Judas

Jesus said, "[Come] and I'll teach you about the [mysteries that no] human [will] ever see. There exists a great and boundless realm whose horizons no angelic generation has seen. That's where a [great] invisible Spirit is, which no [angelic] eye has ever seen, no heart has ever comprehended, and it's never been called by any name.

"A luminous cloud appeared there. The Spirit said, 'Let an angel come into existence to attend me.' Then a great angel, the Self-Begotten, the God of the Light, emerged from the cloud. Because of him, another four angels came into existence from another cloud, and they attended the angelic Self-Begotten. **48** 'Let [a realm] come into existence,' the [Self-Begotten] said, and it came into existence [just as he said]. He [created] the first luminary to rule over it. Next he said, 'Let angels come into existence to serve [it,' and myriads] without number came into existence. He said, '[Let a] luminous realm come into existence,' and it came into existence. He created the second luminary to rule over it, along with myriads of angels without number to offer service. That's how he created the rest of the realms of light. He made them to be ruled, and created for them myriads of angels without number to assist them.

"The spiritual Adam was in the first cloud of light that no angel could ever see among all those called 'God.' **49** And [the spiritual Adam fathered Seth in] that [place after the] image [of ...] and after the likeness of [this] angel. He made the incorruptible [generation] of Seth appear to the twelve androgynous [luminaries. Then] he made seventy-two luminaries appear in the incorruptible generation according to the Spirit's will. The seventy-two luminaries themselves made three hundred sixty luminaries appear in the incorruptible generation according to the Spirit's will so that there'd be five for each. The twelve realms of the twelve luminaries make up their father, with six heavens for each realm so there are seventy-two heavens for the seventy-two luminaries, and for each one **50** there are [five] skies [for a total of] three hundred sixty [skies in all. They] were given authority and a [great] army of angels without number for honor and service, along with virgin spirits

The Gospel of Judas: The Sarcastic Gospel

[too] for the honor and [service] of all the realms and the heavens with their skies.

"Now the crowd of those immortals is called 'cosmos' or 'perishable' by the father and the seventy-two luminaries with the Self-Begotten and his seventy-two realms. That's where the first human appeared with his incorruptible powers. In the realm that appeared with his generation is the cloud of knowledge and the angel called **51** [Eleleth ...] After that [Eleleth] said, 'Let twelve angels come into existence [to] rule over Chaos and [Hades]. And look, from the cloud there appeared an [angel] whose face flashed with [fire] and whose likeness was [defiled] by blood. His name was Nebro, which means 'Rebel.' Others call him Yaldabaoth. Another angel, Saklas, came from the cloud too. So Nebro created six angels – and Saklas (did too) – to be assistants. They brought out twelve angels in the heavens, with each of them receiving a portion in the heavens.

"And the twelve rulers spoke with the twelve angels: 'Let each of you **52** [...] and let them [...] generation [... five] angels:

The first [is Yaoth], who's called 'the Good One.'

The second is Harmathoth, [the eye of fire].

The [third] is Galila.

The fourth [is] Yobel.

The fifth is Adonaios.

These are the five who ruled over Hades and are the first over Chaos.

"Then Saklas told his angels, 'Let's create a human being after the likeness and the image.' And they fashioned Adam and his wife Eve, who in the cloud is called 'Life,' because by this name all the generations seek him, and each of them calls her by their names. Now Saklas didn't **53** [command ...] give birth, except [...] among the generations [...] which this [...] and the [angel] told him, 'Your life will last for a limited time, with your children.'"

"[How] long can a person live?" Judas asked Jesus.

Jesus asked, "Why are you amazed that the lifespans of Adam and his generation are limited in the place he's received his kingdom with his ruler?"

"Does the human spirit die?" Judas asked Jesus.

"This is how it is," Jesus said. "God commanded Michael to loan spirits to people so that they might serve. Then the Great One commanded Gabriel to give spirits to the great generation with no king – the spirit along with the soul. So the [rest] of the souls **54** […] light [… the] Chaos […] seek [the] spirit within you which you've made to live in this flesh from the angelic generations. God caused knowledge to be brought to Adam and those with him, so that the kings of Chaos and Hades might not lord it over them."

[Then] Judas asked Jesus, "What will those generations do?"

"Truly I tell you," Jesus said, "the stars complete all these things. When Saklas completes the time span that's been determined for him, their first star will appear with the generations, and they'll finish what's been said. Then they'll sleep around in my name, murder their children, **55** and [they'll …] evil and […] the realms, bringing the generations and presenting them to Saklas. [And] after that […] will bring its twelve tribes of [Israel] from […], and the [generations] will all serve Saklas, sinning in my name. And your star will [rule] over the thirteenth realm." Then Jesus [laughed].

"Master," [Judas] asked, "Why [are you laughing at me]?"

In response [Jesus told him], "I'm not laughing [at you but] at the error of the stars, because these six stars go astray with these five warriors, and they'll all be destroyed along with their creations."

Then Judas asked Jesus, "What will those people do who've been baptized in your name?"

The Betrayal

"Truly I tell [you]," Jesus said, "this baptism **56** [which they've received in] my name […] will destroy the whole

The Gospel of Judas: The Sarcastic Gospel

generation of the earthly Adam. Tomorrow they'll torture the one who bears me. Truly I [tell] you, no hand of a mortal human [will hurt] me. Truly [I tell] you, Judas, those who offer sacrifices to Saklas [...] everything that's evil. But you'll do more than all of them, because you'll sacrifice the humanity which bears me. Your horn has already been raised, your anger has been kindled, your star has ascended, and your heart has [strayed]. **57** Truly [I tell you], your last [... and] the [... the thrones] of the realm have [been defeated], the kings have grown weak, the angelic generations have grieved, the evil [they sowed ...] is destroyed, [and] the [ruler] is wiped out. [And] then the [fruit] of the great generation of Adam will be exalted, because before heaven, earth, and the angels, that generation from the realms exists. Look, you've been told everything. Look up and see the cloud with the light in it and the stars around it. The star that leads the way is your star."

So Judas looked up and saw the luminous cloud, and he entered it. Those standing on the ground heard a voice from the cloud saying, **58** "[... the] great [generation ...] and [...]." And Judas didn't see Jesus anymore.

Immediately there was a disturbance among [the] Jews, more than [...] Their high priests grumbled because he'd gone into the guest room to pray. But some scribes were there watching closely so they could arrest him during his prayer, because they were afraid of the people, since they all regarded him as a prophet.

They approached Judas and asked him, "What are you doing here? Aren't you Jesus' disciple?"

He told them what they wanted to hear. Then Judas received some money and handed him over to them.

The Gospel
of Judas

The Gospel of Judas: The Sarcastic Gospel

7
The Question of "Gnosticism"

Several scholars, including Ehrman, Wright, DeConick, and many others, agree that Judas' Gospel is a "Gnostic" text.[1] Historically, "Gnosticism" has been widely believed to be an early rival movement within the developing institutional church, often regarded as a Christian "heresy." However, the previous consensus about "Gnosticism" has begun to unravel in recent years.

The history behind this controversy is too long and involved to be detailed here, but perhaps a brief description will suffice.

From the second to the fourth century, as Christianity developed and struggled to define itself, Jesus' followers often engaged in heated arguments over a wide variety of viewpoints. The "Church Fathers" whose viewpoints eventually prevailed essentially won the war of words using familiar rhetorical strategies. In order to define "orthodox" ("true") Christianity, they singled out others as "heretics."

Some of the key "heresy hunters" (or "heresiologists") included Irenaeus of Lyons, Hippolytus of Rome, Tertullian of Carthage, and Epiphanius of Salamis. By lumping together a variety of opposing viewpoints and labeling those who held them under broad categories, they effectively defined the terms of the debate. Their efforts were so successful, in fact, that historians and scholars are still struggling to understand who the different dialogue partners were and what they really believed.

The term "Gnosticism" is in fact a relatively recent label used to describe a broad range of ancient beliefs. The word

40

The Gospel of Judas: The Sarcastic Gospel

"Gnostic," which is an ancient label, comes from the Greek word *gnōsis*, which means "knowledge."

The beliefs of the Gnostics are said to include a cluster of ideas stemming from a dualistic view of spirit and matter – spirit being inherently good and matter being inherently evil. If the physical creation is inherently evil, it must have been created by the inferior, ignorant "craftsman" or "demiurge" who enslaved good spirits in the prison of human bodies. Additionally, since matter is inherently evil, Jesus could not have been truly human and therefore could not really have died on the cross or have risen from the dead as traditional Christianity has maintained. The ethical implications of these teachings were believed to lead to erroneous extremes: either an "ascetic" ethic that all material pleasure is also evil, or a "libertine" ethic that since matter is inherently evil, whatever spiritual people do in the flesh doesn't matter anyway.

This definition of what is "Gnostic," however, seems problematic on many levels.

For one thing, although the letters attributed to Paul warn against "the empty chatter and opposing ideas of so-called knowledge" (*gnōseōs*, 1 Tim. 6:20, DFV), they also explain that in Christ "all the treasures of wisdom and knowledge (*gnōseōs*) are hidden" (Col. 2:3, DFV). Similarly, Clement of Alexandria famously describes the true "Gnostic, who is after the image and likeness of God, who imitates God as far as possible" (*Strom.* II.19). So in some of these early Christian texts, it's not even clear whether being considered a "Gnostic" is such a bad thing after all.

Consequently, some have suggested distinguishing between "Gnostic" and "Gnosticism" or between "gnostic" (with a small "g") and "Gnostic" (with a capital "G"), with the latter implying the detailed dualistic system described above and the former implying spiritual knowledge more consistent with historic Christian faith.[2] But such a distinction still suggests that there's a clearly defined belief system which can be isolated and identified as "Gnosticism," an idea due in large measure to the works of the heresiologists.

Up until the 20th century, almost all of the writings of the "Gnostics" in question were available only in quotations preserved by the heresiologists. In 1945, however, an entire library of previously unknown Coptic texts was discovered near Nag Hammadi in Egypt. For the first time, scholars had at their disposal first-hand accounts of some of the people whom the heresiologists described as heretics.

Initially interpreters read these documents in light of the heresiologists' descriptions. However, some have raised questions about the traditional categories. Influential scholars like Karen King have raised so many questions about the traditional narrative[3] that some have even called for a moratorium on the use of the label "Gnosticism."[4] Michael Allen Williams has highlighted the fact that the texts in collections like the Nag Hammadi Library and the Codex Tchacos (which includes the Gospel of Judas) do not all represent the same viewpoint. In fact, none of these Coptic texts individually contains all the teachings described above as key ideas unique to "Gnosticism," and often those clichés are simply read into the texts.[5] Judas' Gospel is no exception.

On the one hand, Judas' Gospel does teach that the physical creation was the work of an evil demiurge, but the ethics of this Gospel are neither ascetic nor libertine. For example, in its censure of institutional church leaders on page 38, this Gospel is just as critical of fasting as it is of promiscuity. Nor does it deny the crucifixion, which Jesus predicts on page 56.[6]

But does it deny the humanity (and consequently the suffering and death) of Jesus when it portrays Jesus as telling Judas that "you'll sacrifice the human who bears me"? (p. 56, Public Domain Version). Not necessarily — it may be anachronistic to read fifth-century debates about the divinity and humanity of Christ back into the second century, when Christians were just beginning to struggle with how to describe the spiritual nature of Jesus in contemporary philosophical terms. In his doctoral dissertation on Judas' Gospel, Lance Jenott cites other early Christians who used similar language to describe Jesus' "two natures," including Melito of Sardis, Tertullian of Carthage, Athanasius, and others.[7]

Interestingly, another book in the same codex, *The Letter of Peter to Philip*, states that Jesus "died for us" (p. 7) and that "he rose from the dead" (p. 8), precisely what "Gnostics" are said not to have believed. This isn't to deny that sometimes there really are significant differences between canonical scriptures and some of these so-called "Gnostic" scriptures, but it is to suggest that many scholars (both those who dismiss them as "heretical" and those who seem to prefer them to canonical scriptures) have sometimes overstated these differences.

Nevertheless, this leaves an unanswered question. If these other traditions aren't "Gnostic," then what are they? There is no consensus on this point. Williams suggests a more descriptive label: "biblical demiurgical," a term which would focus attention on an actual feature of many of these texts without reinforcing old clichés and unfounded caricatures.[8] This label, however, doesn't appear to have caught on. Personally, I'm hesitant to take up a label with too many syllables and with terms (like "demiurge") that most people aren't familiar with. I also tend to be hesitant about trying to make up labels generally.

Is there a better way, then, to describe these texts – in a way that doesn't lump them all together (whether they belong together or not) and misrepresent them, a way that may better reflect the self-understanding of the people who actually wrote and read these texts? I think that there is.

Scholars who study "Gnosticism" already distinguish between different types of "Gnosticism," such as "Valentinian Gnosticism" (a belief system taught by disciples of the second-century bishop Valentinus) and "Sethian Gnosticism" (so called because of the prominence of the biblical character Seth in these texts). If we simply drop the terms "Gnostic" and "Gnosticism" and describe certain texts as "Valentinian" or "Sethian" based on their contents, it may be easier to consider them in their own contexts without reading into them things that aren't really there.

Based in large part on its description of the heavenly realm, Judas' Gospel is clearly related to a number of texts which provide a similar description using many of the same names ("great invisible Spirit," "Barbelo," "Self-Begotten," "Adamas," "Nebro," "Yaldabaoth," "Saklas," and so on) and which generally highlight "the incorruptible generation of Seth." So it is fair to describe Judas' Gospel as belonging to a category of recognizable "Sethian" texts that have many features in common.[9]

When Sethian texts are lumped together with less similar texts under the rubric of "Gnosticism," however, they tend to be forced into a uniform mold, interpreted in light of a system artificially created by taking pieces from individual texts and building a metanarrative into which to cram all the pieces, ignoring the differences between them. The way they're categorized, then, determines the metanarrative that's superimposed over them both collectively and individually. Interestingly, this same dynamic explains the current "canon" of Christian scripture.

The Gospel of Judas: The Sarcastic Gospel

8
The "Canon" of Scripture

The gradual replacement of scrolls by codices in the second through the fourth centuries helped to drive the development of a Christian "canon" of scripture,[1] creating an important relationship between individual "books" and "the Book" which contains them. When multiple stories can be written down in one larger book, which ones should be included? Which should come first? What order should they be placed in? The order in which the books are arranged tends to create an organized framework in which the individual books are understood, arguably creating another layer of meaning.

For example, the canonical New Testament's books clearly aren't arranged in the order in which they were written. Instead, the New Testament opens with four Gospels featuring the life of Jesus. They're followed in turn by the book of Acts, which narrates the development of an organized church overseen by his disciples, then by a series of letters, and finally a concluding Apocalypse. Paul's letters to various churches (the earliest New Testament texts) are actually framed on one side by Acts – which outlines a narrative downplaying differences between Paul and the other apostles – and on the other side by letters attributed to the other apostles themselves, automatically suggesting reading strategies to interpret these texts in the light of one another.

Significantly, different churches and communities of faith have different "canons" of scripture. For example, the "Old Testament" books of Orthodox, Catholic, and Protestant Bibles are arranged very differently than those in the Tanakh, the Jewish Bible. The Jewish Bible, like the Christian Old

The Gospel of Judas: The Sarcastic Gospel

Testament, begins with the first five books of Moses (starting with Genesis), but unlike the Christian Old Testament, the Tanakh culminates in 2 Chronicles, ending on a note of fulfillment – the announcement of the end of Israel's exile (2 Chron. 36:22,23). By contrast, the Christian Old Testament ends with the prophet Malachi, ending on a note of expectation and the divine promise "to send you Elijah the prophet before the coming of the great and terrible day of the LORD" (Mal. 4:5, NRSV). The next book in the Christian Bible is Matthew's Gospel, which features John the Baptist in terms reminiscent of Malachi as a way of introducing Jesus (cf. Matt. 11:14; Mark 9:13). In the Christian canon of scripture, then, "the Old Testament" leads seamlessly to "the New Testament" in an unbroken sequence.

The Catholic canon is larger than the Protestant canon, including what Protestants consider "apocrypha," books from the Greek translation of the Tanakh (known as the Septuagint) which was completed by the second century BCE. Eastern Orthodox churches include even more. So the Jewish canon contains twenty-four books in its collection; the Protestant canon contains sixty-six; the Catholic canon contains seventy-three; and the Orthodox canon contains seventy-eight. More recent Christian organizations boast even more, such as the Church of Jesus Christ of the Latter Day Saints, which includes the sixty-six books of the Protestant canon plus the Book of Mormon, the Doctrine and Covenants, and the Pearl of Great Price.

From time to time people ask me whether I think Gospels like Mary and Thomas should be included in the New Testament canon. I regard the question as hypothetical rather than practical. True, there are some newer versions of the New Testament, like *The Restored New Testament*[2] and *The New New Testament*,[3] which do include some of these early Christian texts; but simply publishing a few extra texts alongside New Testament books doesn't make them "canonical." What makes a text "canonical" is its shared use by members of a community of

The Gospel of Judas: The Sarcastic Gospel

faith who consider it to be a formative spiritual text, a divinely-inspired writing with the power to transform us into the people we were originally intended to be. Unless church organizations begin broadening their liturgies to include material from other Gospels, they will not ever be "canonical" texts.

That's not to say that these Gospels can't be read alongside canonical Gospels, or that they can't complement canonical texts in an individual's spiritual quest for divine enlightenment. It's simply to acknowledge that communities of faith haven't historically accorded them a place of privilege alongside other revered texts.

I like to think of it in terms of three "C"s of Christian definition. Traditionally, these three "C"s have been understood as creed, canon, and clergy, with each reinforcing the other. However, I think of Christian self-understanding in terms of a different three "C"s – that is, "Christ-centered communities." Creeds, canons, and clerical authority differ between Christian institutions, but irrespective of models of authority, all are shaped by the shared experiences of their members. And I believe that in actual practice, this has been true throughout the entire history of the church.

The canonical books of the Christian New Testament are foundational spiritual texts for Christians, but they are not the only texts written by early Christians. They document the spread of the Christian message through Greece to Rome (where it eventually developed into the dominant form of Christianity), but they don't describe the initial spread of Christianity south into Egypt and east into Syria and beyond.[4]

Gospels like Mary and Thomas were written and copied in these other environments. Like the New Testament's Gospels, they can be read in more than one context. Though these Gospels were originally written in Greek during the second century, they were translated into Coptic in later centuries and included in codices alongside other types of texts, including Sethian ones (like the Secret Book of John), suggesting certain interpretative frameworks possibly foreign to their original context.[5] But they can be read in other contexts, too, including the canonical New Testament's context.

Other Gospels, like Judas' Gospel, may be more difficult to read within the context of the New Testament's canon, but they are all nevertheless valuable as testaments to diverse beliefs throughout the world of late antiquity – including diverse beliefs among a wide variety of people seeking to follow Jesus as best they could.

The Gospel of Judas: The Sarcastic Gospel

Appendix
A Public Domain Version of the Gospel of Judas

The translation of Judas' Gospel presented in this Appendix has been committed to the public domain. It may be freely copied and used, in whole or in part, changed or unchanged, for any purpose.

The text is based on the Codex Tchacos, page 33 through page 58 (TC, *3*, 33 - 58). It's a fourth-century Coptic translation of an earlier Greek text dating to the middle of the second century (prior to 180 CE), which would mean it was written shortly after the latest books of the New Testament. It was discovered in Egypt in the 1970s but languished in obscurity in the antiquities market for decades before it was finally purchased by Frieda Tchacos Nussberger on April 3, 2000 and responsibly restored, translated, and initially published six years later.

The text in Codex Tchacos, which remains our only known copy of this Gospel to date, is still missing several fragments. The fragments which became available after the publication of National Geographic's critical edition have been included in this translation, but many gaps in the manuscript remain. These gaps are indicated in the translation by brackets, and all words in brackets are proposed reconstructions. Words in parentheses are strictly editorial insertions to clarify the meaning of the text.

This translation is based on the following Coptic transcripts:

Kasser, Rodolphe, and Wurst, Gregor, *The Gospel of Judas, Critical Edition: Together with the Letter of Peter to Philip, James, and a Book of Allogenes from Codex Tchacos* (National Geographic), 2007, pp. 185-235

The Gospel of Judas: The Sarcastic Gospel

Wurst, Gregor, *"Addenda Et Corrigenda* to the Critcial Edition of the *Gospel of Judas," in* DeConick, April D., ed., *The Codex Judas Papers: Proceedings of the International Congress on the Tchacos Codex held at Rice University, Houston, Texas, March 13-16, 2008* (Brill), 2009, pp. 503-507

Krosney, Herbert, Meyer, Marvin, and Wurst, Gregor, "Preliminary Report on New Fragments of Codex Tchacos" *Early Christianity* 1 (2010), pp. 282-294

Jenott, Lance, *The Gospel of Judas: Coptic Text, Translation, and Historical Interpretation of the 'Betrayer's Gospel'* (Mohr Siebeck), 2011, pp. 134-187

Introduction

33 This is the secret message of judgment Jesus spoke with Judas Iscariot over a period of eight days, three days before he celebrated Passover.

When he appeared on earth, he did signs and great wonders for the salvation of humanity. Some [walked] in the way of righteousness, but others walked in their transgression, so the twelve disciples were called. He started to tell them about the mysteries beyond the world and what would happen at the end. Often he didn't reveal himself to his disciples, but you'd find him in their midst as a child.

Jesus Criticizes The Disciples

One day he was with his disciples in Judea. He found them sitting together practicing their piety. When he [came up to] his disciples **34** sitting together praying over the bread, [he] laughed.

The disciples said to him, "Master, why are you laughing at [our] prayer? What have we done? [This] is what's right."

He answered and said to them, "I'm not laughing at you. You're not doing this because you want to, but because through this your God [will be] praised."

They said, "Master, you [...] are the Son of our God!"

Jesus said to them, "How do [you] know me? Truly [I] say to you, no generation of the people among you will know me."

When his disciples heard this, [they] started to get angry and furious and started to curse him in their hearts.

But when Jesus noticed their ignorance, [he said] to them, "Why are you letting your anger trouble you? Has your God within you and [his stars] **35** become angry with your souls? If any of you is [strong enough] among humans to bring out the perfect Humanity, stand up and face me."

All of them said, "We're strong enough." But their spirits weren't brave enough to stand before [him] – except Judas Iscariot. He was able to stand before him, but he couldn't look him in the eye, so he looked away.

Judas [said] to him, "I know who you are and where you've come from. You've come from the immortal realm of Barbelo, and I'm not worthy to utter the name of the one who's sent you."

Then Jesus, knowing that he was thinking about what's exalted, said to him, "Come away from the others and I'll tell you the mysteries of the kingdom. Not so that you'll go there, but you'll grieve much **36** because someone else will replace you to complete the twelve [elements] before their God."

Judas said to him, "When will you tell me these things, and when will the great day of light dawn for the generation [...]?"

But when he said these things, Jesus left him.

Another Generation

The next morning, he appeared to his disciples. [And] they said to him, "Master, where did [you] go and what did you do when you left us?"

Jesus said to them, "I went to another great and holy generation."

His disciples said to him, "Lord, what great generation is better and holier than us, that's not in these realms?"

Now when Jesus heard this, he laughed. He said to them, "Why are you wondering in your hearts about the strong and holy generation? **37** Truly I say to you, no one born [of] this realm will see that [generation], no army of angels from the stars will rule over it, and no person of mortal birth will be able to join it, because that generation doesn't come from […] that has become […] the generation of the people among [them] is from the generation of the great people […] the powerful authorities who […] nor the powers […] those by which you rule."

When his disciples heard these things, they were each troubled in their spirit. They couldn't say a thing.

The Disciples' Vision

Another day Jesus came up to them. They said to him, "Master, we've seen you in a dream, because we had great [dreams last] night."

But Jesus said, "Why […] hidden yourselves?"

38 And they [said, "We saw] a great [house, with a great] altar [in it, and] twelve people – we'd say they were priests – and a name. And a crowd of people was waiting at the altar [until] the priests [finished receiving] the offerings. We kept waiting too."

[Jesus said], "What were they like?"

And they said, "[Some] fast [for] two weeks. Others sacrifice their own children; others their wives, praising and humbling themselves among each other. Others sleep with men; others murder; yet others commit many sins and do criminal things. [And] the people standing [before] the altar invoke your [name]! **39** And in all their sacrificing, they fill the [altar] with their offerings." When they said this, [they] fell silent because they were troubled.

The Gospel of Judas: The Sarcastic Gospel

Jesus said to them, "Why are you troubled? Truly I say to you, all the priests standing before that altar invoke my name. And [again], I say to you, my name has been written on this [house] of the generations of the stars by the human generations. [And they] have shamefully planted fruitless trees in my name." Jesus said to them, "You're the ones receiving the offerings on the altar you've seen. That's the God you serve, and you're the twelve people you've seen. And the animals you saw brought in to be sacrificed are the crowd you lead astray **40** before that altar. [Your minister] will stand up and use my name like that, and [the] generations of the pious will be loyal to him. After him, another person will present [those who sleep around], and another those who murder children, and another those who sleep with men, and those who fast, and the rest of impurity, crime, and error. And those who say, 'We're equal to the angels' – they're the stars that finish everything. It's been said to the human generations, 'Look, God has accepted your sacrifice from the hands of priests,' that is, the minister of error. But the Lord who commands is the Lord over everything. On the last day, they'll be found guilty."

41 Jesus said [to them], "Stop [sacrificing animals]. You've [offered them] over the altar, over your stars with your angels where they've already been completed. So let them become [...] with you and let them [become] clear."

His disciples [said to him], "Cleanse us from our [sins] that we've committed through the deceit of the angels."

Jesus said to them, "It's not possible [...], nor [can] a fountain quench the fire of the entire inhabited world. Nor can a [city's] well satisfy all the generations, except the great, stable one. A single lamp won't illuminate all the realms, except the second generation, nor can a baker feed all creation **42** under [heaven]."

And [when the disciples heard] these [things], they said to [him], "Master, help us and save us!"

Jesus said to them, "Stop struggling against me. Each one of you has his own star, [and ...] of the stars will [...] what belongs to it [...] I wasn't sent to the corruptible generation, but to the strong and incorruptible generation, because no enemy has ruled [over] that generation, nor any of the stars. Truly I say to you, the pillar of fire will fall quickly and that generation won't be moved by the stars."

Jesus and Judas

And when Jesus [said] these things, he left, [taking] Judas Iscariot with him. He said to him, "The water on the exalted mountain is [from] **43** [...] it didn't come to [water ... the well] of the tree of [the fruit ...] of this realm [...] after a time [...], but came to water God's paradise and the enduring [fruit], because [it] won't corrupt that generation's [walk of life], but [it will exist] for all eternity."

Judas said to [him, "Tell] me, what kind of fruit does this generation have?"

Jesus said, "The souls of every human generation will die; however, when these people have completed the time in the kingdom and the spirit leaves them, their bodies will die but their souls will live, and they'll be taken up."

Judas said, "What will the rest of the human generations do?"

Jesus said, "It's not possible **44** to sow on [rock] and harvest its fruit. In the same way, it's [not possible to sow on] the [defiled] race along with the perishable wisdom [and] the hand which created mortal humans so that their souls may go up to the realms above. [Truly] I say to you, [no ruler], angel, [or] power will be able to see the [places] that [this great], holy generation [will see]." When Jesus said this, he left.

Judas said, "Master, just as you've listened to all of them, now listen to me too, because I've seen a great vision."

But Jesus laughed when he heard this. He said to him, "Why are you all worked up, you thirteenth demon? But speak up, and I'll bear with you."

Judas said to him, "In the vision, I saw myself. The twelve disciples are stoning me and **45** chasing [me rapidly]. And I also came to the place where [I had followed] you. I saw [a house in this place], and my eyes couldn't [measure] its size. Great people surrounded it, and that house had a roof of greenery. In the middle of the house was [a crowd ...]. Master, take me in with these people!"

[Jesus] answered and said, "Your star has led you astray, Judas," and that "no person of mortal birth is worthy to enter the house you've seen, because that place is reserved for those who are holy. Neither the sun nor the moon will rule there, nor the day, but those who are holy will always stand in the realm with the holy angels. Look, I've told you the mysteries of the kingdom **46** and I've taught you about the error of the stars and [...] sent [on high] over the twelve realms."

Judas said, "Master, surely my seed doesn't dominate the rulers, does it?"

Jesus answered and said to him, "Come, let me [tell] you [about the holy generation. Not so that you'll go there], but you'll grieve much when you see the kingdom and all its generation."

When Judas heard this, he said to him, "What good has it done me that you've separated me from that generation?"

Jesus answered and said, "You'll become the thirteenth, and will be cursed by the other generations and will rule over them. In the last days they'll [...] to you and you won't go up **47** to the holy generation."

Jesus Reveals Everything to Judas

Jesus said, "[Come] and I'll teach you about the [mysteries that no] human [will] see, because there exists a great and boundless realm whose horizons no angelic generation has seen, [in] which is a [great] invisible Spirit, which no [angelic] eye has ever seen, no heart has ever comprehended, and it's never been called by any name.

The Gospel of Judas: The Sarcastic Gospel

"And a luminous cloud appeared there. And he (the Spirit) said, 'Let an angel come into being to attend me.' And a great angel, the Self-Begotten, the God of the Light, emerged from the cloud. And because of him, another four angels came into being from another cloud, and they attended the angelic Self-Begotten. And said **48** the [Self-Begotten], 'Let [a realm] come into being,' and it came into being [just as he said]. And he [created] the first luminary to rule over it. And he said, 'Let angels come into being to serve [it,' and myriads] without number came into being. And he said, '[Let a] luminous realm come into being,' and it came into being. He created the second luminary to rule over it, along with myriads of angels without number to offer service. And that's how he created the rest of the realms of light. And he made them to be ruled, and created for them myriads of angels without number to assist them.

"And Adamas was in the first cloud of light that no angel could ever see among all those called 'God.' **49** And [Adamas begat Seth in] that [place after the] image [of ...] and after the likeness of [this] angel. He made the incorruptible [generation] of Seth appear to the twelve androgynous [luminaries. And then] he made seventy-two luminaries appear in the incorruptible generation according to the Spirit's will. Then the seventy-two luminaries themselves made three hundred sixty luminaries appear in the incorruptible generation according to the Spirit's will so that there'd be five for each. And the twelve realms of the twelve luminaries make up their father, with six heavens for each realm so there are seventy-two heavens for the seventy-two luminaries, and for each one **50** [of them five] firmaments [for a total of] three hundred sixty [firmaments. They] were given authority and a [great] army of angels without number for honor and service, along with virgin spirits [too] for the honor and [service] of all the realms and the heavens with their firmaments.

"Now the crowd of those immortals is called 'cosmos' – that is, 'perishable' – by the father and the seventy-two luminaries with the Self-Begotten and his seventy-two realms. That's where the first human appeared with his incorruptible powers. In the realm that appeared with his generation is the cloud of knowledge and the angel who's called **51** [Eleleth ...] After these things [Eleleth] said, 'Let twelve angels come into being [to] rule over Chaos and [Hades]. And look, from the cloud there appeared an [angel] whose face flashed with [fire] and whose likeness was [defiled] by blood. His name was Nebro, which means 'Rebel.' Others call him Yaldabaoth. And another angel, Saklas, came from the cloud too. So Nebro created six angels – and Saklas (did too) – to be assistants. They brought out twelve angels in the heavens, with each of them receiving a portion in the heavens.

"And the twelve rulers spoke with the twelve angels: 'Let each of you **52** [...] and let them [...] generation [... five] angels:

The first [is Yaoth], who's called 'the Good One.'

The second is Harmathoth, [the eye of fire].

The [third] is Galila.

The fourth [is] Yobel.

The fifth is Adonaios.

These are the five who ruled over Hades and are the first over Chaos.

"Then Saklas said to his angels, 'Let's create a human being after the likeness and the image.' And they fashioned Adam and his wife Eve, who in the cloud is called 'Life,' because by this name all the generations seek him, and each of them calls her by their names. Now Saklas didn't **53** [command ...] give birth, except [...] among the generations [...] which this [...] and the [angel] said to him, 'Your life will last for a limited time, with your children.'"

Then Judas said to Jesus, "[How] long can a person live?"

Jesus said, "Why are you amazed that the lifespans of Adam and his generation are limited in the place he's received his kingdom with his ruler?"

Judas said to Jesus, "Does the human spirit die?"

Jesus said, "This is how it is. God commanded Michael to loan spirits to people so that they might serve. Then the Great One commanded Gabriel to give spirits to the great generation with no king – the spirit along with the soul. So the [rest] of the souls **54** [...] light [... the] Chaos [...] seek [the] spirit within you which you've made to live in this flesh from the angelic generations. Then God caused knowledge to be brought to Adam and those with him, so that the kings of Chaos and Hades might not rule over them."

[Then] Judas said to Jesus, "So what will those generations do?"

Jesus said, "Truly I say to you, the stars complete all these things. When Saklas completes the time span that's been determined for him, their first star will appear with the generations, and they'll finish what's been said. Then they'll sleep around in my name, murder their children, **55** and [they'll ...] evil and [...] the realms, bringing the generations and presenting them to Saklas. [And] after that [...] will bring the twelve tribes of [Israel] from [...], and the [generations] will all serve Saklas, sinning in my name. And your star will [rule] over the thirteenth realm." Then Jesus [laughed].

[Judas] said, "Master, why [are you laughing at me?"

Jesus] answered [and said], "I'm not laughing [at you but] at the error of the stars, because these six stars go astray with these five warriors, and they'll all be destroyed along with their creations."

Then Judas said to Jesus, "What will those do who've been baptized in your name?"

The Betrayal

Jesus said, "Truly I say [to you], this baptism **56** [which they've received in] my name [...] will destroy the whole generation of the earthly Adam. Tomorrow they'll torture the one who bears me. Truly I [say] to you, no hand of a mortal human [will fall] upon me. Truly [I say] to you, Judas, those who offer sacrifices to Saklas [...] everything that's evil. But you'll do more than all of them, because you'll sacrifice the human who bears me. Your horn has already been raised, your anger has

The Gospel of Judas: The Sarcastic Gospel

been kindled, your star has ascended, and your heart has [strayed]. **57** Truly [I say to you], your last [… and] the [… the thrones] of the realm have [been defeated], the kings have grown weak, the angelic generations have grieved, and the evil [they sowed …] is destroyed, [and] the [ruler] is wiped out. [And] then the [fruit] of the great generation of Adam will be exalted, because before heaven, earth, and the angels, that generation from the realms exists. Look, you've been told everything. Lift up your eyes and see the cloud with the light in it and the stars around it. And the star that leads the way is your star."

Then Judas looked up and saw the luminous cloud, and he entered it. Those standing on the ground heard a voice from the cloud saying, **58** "[… the] great [generation …] and […]." And Judas didn't see Jesus anymore.

Immediately there was a disturbance among [the] Jews, more than […] Their high priests grumbled because he'd gone into the guest room to pray. But some scribes were there watching closely so they could arrest him during his prayer, because they were afraid of the people, since they all regarded him as a prophet.

And they approached Judas and said to him, "What are you doing here? Aren't you Jesus' disciple?"

Then he answered them as they wished. Then Judas received some money and handed him over to them.

The Gospel
of Judas

Text Notes

Page 33: *"Judgment."* Or "declaration."

Page 36: *"Elements."* Rodolphe Kasser and Gregor Wurst reconstruct this word as "disciples" in *The Gospel of Judas, Critical Edition: Together with the Letter of Peter to Philip, James, and a Book of*

Allogenes from Codex Tchacos (National Geographic), 2007, p. 191; but cf. Lance Jenott, *The Gospel of Judas: Coptic Text, Translation, and Historical Interpretation of the 'Betrayer's Gospel'* (Mohr Siebeck), 2011, pp. 54-56; 193-194.

Page 38: *"Receiving."* Kasser and Wurst reconstruct this word as "presenting" *(op. cit.,* p. 195); but cf. Jenott, *op. cit.,* p. 196.

Page 40: *"Your minister."* Kasser and Wurst originally considered "the ruler of the world" as a possible reconstruction *(op. cit.,* p. 199, which is followed by Barnstone; cp. King, "the ruler of chaos"), but they suggested instead reconstructing the gap to read "the bishop" or "the minister" based on what follows. For "your minister," cf. Jenott, *op. cit.,* p. 64. *"Present."* Meyer and Gaudard translate "stand up from," King translates "stand with," and DeConick translates "stand up for"; but cf. Jenott, *op. cit.,* pp. 65,66.

Page 44: *"Demon."* Literally, *"daimon,"* translated initially as "spirit" by Meyer and later as "god" by King. In broader Greek literature, *daimons* weren't necessarily evil spirits, but in Jewish and Christian literature, they were unambiguously regarded as evil. Cf. Birger A. Pearson, "Judas Iscariot in the *Gospel of Judas,"* in *The Codex Judas Papers: Proceedings of the International Congress on the Tchacos Codex held at Rice University, Houston, Texas, March 13-16, 2008,* ed. by April D. DeConick (Brill), 2009, pp. 138-140.

Page 45: *"A roof of greenery."* Or possibly *"a roof of lightning"* or *"fire."* Cf. Lance Jenott, "The *Gospel of Judas* 45,6-7 and Enoch's Heavenly Temple," in *The Codex Judas Papers, op. cit.,* pp. 471-477.

Page 46: *"Surely my seed doesn't dominate the rulers, does it?"* Following King, DeConick, and Jenott. Meyer and Gaudard translate, "could it be that my seed is under the control of the rulers?" and Barnstone, "could my seed, my heritage, fall under the control of the archons, who are rulers of this world?"

Page 47 and following: *"The Self-Begotten."* Literally, *"Autogenes."*

Page 48: *"Let a realm come into being."* Kasser and Wurst reconstruct "Let A[damas] come into being" *(op. cit., p. 215)*; but cf. Jenott, *Judas, op. cit.,* pp. 80-84.

Page 49: *"The twelve androgynous luminaries."* Kasser and Wurst reconstruct "the twelve […] 24 […]" *(op. cit., p. 217)*; but cf. Jenott, *op. cit.,* pp. 86-87.

Page 51: *"Eleleth."* Cf. Jenott, *op. cit.,* pp. 94ff.

Page 52: *"The first is Yaoth, the one known as 'The Good One.'"* Meyer and Gaudard, King, and Barnstone translate *"The first is Seth, the one who is called the Christ."* However, the context makes that reconstruction doubtful, as the Sethian Christ is never counted among the lower angels. Consequently, this translation follows Jenott's reconstruction of "[Ya]oth" instead of "[Se]th" (cf. Chapter Five, note 3) and DeConick's reading of the sacred abbreviation *"chs"* as *"chrestos"* ("good one") instead of *"christos"* ("Christ"; cf. DeConick, *op cit.,* p. 121).

Page 57: *"Fruit."* Kasser and Wurst propose the reconstruction "image" instead of "fruit" *(op. cit., p. 233)*; but cf. Jenott, *op. cit.,* pp. 33,34.

The Gospel of Judas: The Sarcastic Gospel

Notes

Introduction

[1] Cf. Stephanie Pappas, "Truth Behind Gospel of Judas Revealed in Ancient Inks," *LiveScience,* April 8, 2013, on-line at http://www.livescience.com/28506-gospel-judas-ink-authenticity.html, last accessed May 3, 2014.

[2] Cf. Mark M. Mattison, *The Gospel of Mary: A Fresh Translation and Holistic Approach* (CreateSpace Independent Publishing Platform), 2013, pp. 7-9. See also Chapter Eight.

[3] Cf. Mattison, *ibid.,* p. 53.

[4] Bentley Layton, *Coptic in 20 Lessons: Introduction to Sahidic Coptic With Exercises and Vocabularies* (Peeters), 2007, p. 1.

[5] Cf. Herbert Krosney, Marvin Meyer, and Gregor Wurst, "Preliminary Report on New Fragments of Codex Tchacos" *Early Christianity* 1 (2010), pp. 282-294.

Chapter One

[1] Cf. Mark 3:19; Matt. 10:4; Luke 6:16; John 6:71.

[2] Cf. Mark 14:10,11; Matt. 26:14-16; Luke 22:3-6.

[3] Cf. Mark 14:3-9; Matt. 26:6-13.

[4] Cf. Bart D. Ehrman, *The Lost Gospel of Judas Iscariot: A New Look at Betrayer and Betrayed* (Oxford University Press), 2006, pp. 25,26.

[5] Cf. Luke 22:2; John 13:27.

[6] Cf. Mark 14:18-21; Matt. 26:21-25; Luke 22:21-23; John 13:21-30.

[7] Cf. Mark 14:44-46; Matt. 26:48-50; Luke 22:47,48.

[8] Cf. Matt. 27:3-5; Acts 1:18,19.

[9] Cf. Mark 8:33; Matthew 16:23.

[10] Cf. Mark 14:29,31; Matt. 26:33,35; Luke 22:33; John 13:37.

[11] Cf. Mark 14:30; Matt. 26:34; Luke 22:34; John 13:38.

[12] Cf. Mark 14:21; Matt. 26:24.

[13] Cf. Ehrman, *op cit.*, pp. 44-51.

Chapter Two

[1] Cf. Jean-Yves Leloup, *Judas and Jesus: Two Faces of a Single Revelation* (Inner Traditions), 2007, pp. 151,152.

[2] Cf. Ehrman, *op. cit.*, pp. 62-65.

Chapter Three

[1] Elaine Pagels and Karen L. King, *Reading Judas: The Gospel of Judas and the Shaping of Christianity* (Viking), 2007, p. 3.

[2]Rodolphe Kasser and Wurst, Gregor, *The Gospel of Judas, Critical Edition: Together with the Letter of Peter to Philip, James, and a Book of Allogenes from Codex Tchacos* (National Geographic), 2007, p. 24.

[3]Ehrman, *op. cit.*, p. 138; cf. also Willis Barnstone, *The Restored New Testament: A New Translation with Commentary, Including the Gnostic Gospels Thomas, Mary, and Judas* (W.W. Norton & Company), 2009, p. 591.

[4]April D. DeConick, *The Thirteenth Apostle: What the Gospel of Judas Really Says* (Continuum), 2007, rev. ed. 2009. Cf. also April D. DeConick, "Gospel Truth," *The New York Times*, Op-Ed page, December 1, 2007, on-line at:
http://www.nytimes.com/2007/12/01/opinion/01deconink.html, last accessed May 3, 2014.

[5]Ehrman, *op. cit.*, pp. 97,98; cf. also Marvin Meyer, ed., *The Nag Hammadi Scriptures: The International Edition* (HarperOne), 2008, pp. 755, 769, n. 128.

[6]Cf. Thomas O. Lambdin, *Introduction to Sahidic Coptic* (Mercer University Press), 1983, p. 332.

[7]DeConick, *Thirteenth Apostle, op. cit.*, pp. 61,62.

[8]Kasser and Wurst, *op. cit.*, p. 233.

[9]Krosney, Meyer, and Wurst, *op. cit.*, p. 288.

[10]Cf. DeConick, *Thirteenth Apostle, op. cit.*, pp. 63-65.

[11]Cf. DeConick, *ibid.*, pp. 55,56.

[12]Personal correspondence dated April 27, 2014.

The Gospel of Judas: The Sarcastic Gospel

[13]DeConick, *Thirteenth Apostle, op. cit.,* pp. xx,xi.

[14]DeConick, *ibid.,* p. xx.

[15]DeConick, *ibid.,* p. xix.

[16]Cf. Barnstone, *op. cit.,* p. 593; Ehrman, *op. cit.,* pp. 28, 42-43, 50-51, 138, 144, 180.

[17]Ehrman, *op. cit.,* p. 138.

[18]King and Pagels, *op. cit.,* pp. 99, 165; cf. N.T. Wright, *Judas and the Gospel of Jesus: Have We Missed the Truth about Christianity?* (Baker Books), 2006, pp. 109-118.

Chapter Four

[1]Cynthia Bourgeault, *The Wisdom Jesus: Transforming Heart and Mind – a New Perspective on Christ and His Message* (Shambhala), 2008.

[2]*Ibid.,* p. 185.

[3]*Ibid.,* pp. 185,186.

[4]Leloup, *op. cit.,* pp. 151-157.

[5]Cf. Chapter Seven, n. 9.

[6]Ehrman, *op. cit.,* pp. 134, 137; cf. Deconick: "the twelve disciples are the voice of the apostolic Christians" (*Thirteenth Apostle, op. cit.,* p. 25); Pagels and King: "According to the *Gospel of Judas,* then, the fundamental problem is that "the twelve" – here, stand-ins for church leaders – do not know who Jesus is and do not understand who God is, either" (*op. cit.,* p. 66). Cf.

The Gospel of Judas: The Sarcastic Gospel

also Lance Jenott, *The Gospel of Judas: Coptic Text, Translation, and Historical Interpretation of the 'Betrayer's Gospel'*, (Mohr Siebeck), 2011, pp. 3, 37, 41-43, 68, 131.

[7]Paul's own testimony about his relationship to Jesus' first disciples is much more ambivalent. In one of his first letters, Paul argues from the outset (Gal. 1:1) that his apostleship wasn't grounded in human authority, but was granted directly by Jesus Christ. "I want you to know, sisters and brothers," he wrote, "that the good news I announced is not from human beings. I didn't receive it from human beings, nor was I taught it, but I received it through a revelation of Jesus Christ" (Gal. 1:11,12, DFV). The Jerusalem apostles, Paul wrote, "had nothing for me to add" (Gal. 2:7, DFV). On the other hand, it appears from 1 Corinthians 15:3-9 that Paul wasn't opposed in theory to gospel truth being "passed on" as a tradition from the apostles who had first seen Jesus; his argument was rather that he had seen Jesus directly and had received his apostleship directly from him (1 Cor. 15:8).

[8]DeConick, *Thirteenth Apostle, op. cit.*, p. 111. She goes on to cite Mark 4:37-41; 6:52; 8:15-21,31-33; 9:15-19,33-35; 10:13-14,35-45; 14:50; 16:14. Cf. also Ehrman, *op. cit.*, pp. 18-20.

[9]Cf. Mark 1:24; 3:11; 5:7; cf. DeConick, *ibid.*, pp. 114-116.

[10]Cf. note 7.

[11]Pagels and King, *op. cit.*, pp. 43,44.

[12]At this point N.T. Wright protests that the "orthodox" Christian bishops who embraced martyrdom should hardly be criticized as power-hungry oppressors within the church: "It was

the orthodox Christians who were breaking new ground, and risking their necks as they did so" (*op. cit.*, p. 101). This overlooks a fact which should be familiar to anyone who's ever been part of a minority protest movement – that struggles over authority, and who gets to "represent" the movement, are in fact painfully common.

[13] Cf. Bas van Os, "Stop Sacrificing! The metaphor of sacrifice in the *Gospel of Judas*," in *The Codex Judas Papers: Proceedings of the International Congress on the Tchacos Codex held at Rice University, Houston, Texas, March 13-16, 2008*, ed. by April D. DeConick (Brill), 2009, pp 367-386; Pagels and King, *op. cit.*, pp. 50ff; 65,66; DeConick, *Thirteenth Apostle, op. cit.*, pp. 140-142.

[14] Cf. Jenott, *op. cit.*, pp. 3, 37-41, 44, 47-49, 130.

[15] Cf. Elaine Pagels, "Baptism in the *Gospel of Judas*," in *The Codex Judas Papers, op. cit.*, p. 364.

[16] Cf. Jenott, *op. cit.*, p. 32.

Chapter Five

[1] Cf. Rom. 8:38; 1 Cor. 2:8; Col. 1:16; 2:10,15; 1 Peter 3:22.

[2] Cf. also NHC III, *3*, 84, 12 - 85, 6.

[3] Meyer, King, and Barnstone reconstruct 52, 5 to read "[Se]th" (cf. Kasser and Wurst, *op. cit.*, p. 223), which Meyer admits is an awkward reading given the context (Meyer, *The Nag Hammadi Scriptures, op. cit.*, p. 767, n. 91). This translation follows Jenott's reconstruction of "[Ya]oth" instead of "[Se]th."

[4]The only other possible exception is "the perishable wisdom" mentioned on p. 44.

Chapter Seven

[1]Cf. Ehrman, *op. cit.*, pp. 99-102; Wright, *op. cit.*, pp. 31-35; DeConick, *Thirteenth Apostle, op. cit.*, pp. 26-28.

[2]Cf. Cynthia Bourgeault, *op. cit.*, p. 22.

[3]Cf. Karen King, *What Is Gnosticism?* (Belknap), 2003.

[4]Cf. Cynthia Bourgeault, "Gnosis and Gnosticism," http://www.contemplative.org/pdfs/Gnosis_Gnosticism_CB_April_2010.pdf, last accessed May 3, 2014; Meyer, ed., *The Nag Hammadi Scriptures, op. cit.*, p. 777.

[5]Michael Allen Williams, *Rethinking "Gnosticism": An Argument for Dismantling a Dubious Category* (Princeton University Press), 1996.

[6]Cf. Jenott, *op. cit.*, pp. 23-30.

[7]*Ibid.*, pp. 17-22.

[8]Williams, *op. cit.*, pp. 51-53.

[9]These texts include the Secret Book of John (NHC II, *1*; III, *1*; IV, *1*; BG 8502, *2*), the Reality of the Rulers (NHC II, *4*), the Holy Book of the Great Invisible Spirit (NHC III, *2*; IV, *2*), the Revelation of Adam (NHC V, *5*), the Three Steles of Seth (NHC VII, *5*), Zostrianos (NHC VIII, *1*), Melchizedek (NHC IX, *1*), the Thought of Norea (NHC IX, *2*), Marsanes (NHC X, *1*), Allogenes (NHC XI, *3*), the Trimorphic Protennoia (NHC XIII, *1*), the Book of Allogenes (TC, *4*), the Untitled Text in the

The Gospel of Judas: The Sarcastic Gospel

Bruce Codex, and possibly the Sophia of Jesus Christ (NHC III, *4*; BG 8502, *3*; P. Oxy. 1081). For descriptions, see Appendix 2 in DeConick, *Thirteenth Apostle, op. cit.*, pp. 218-224.

Chapter Eight

[1] Cf. Lee M. McDonald, *The Formation of the Christian Biblical Canon* (Hendrickson Publishers), 1995, p. 115.

[2] Barnstone, *op. cit.*

[3] Hal Taussig, ed., *The New New Testament: A Bible for the 21st Century Combining Traditional and Newly Discovered Texts* (Houghton Mifflin Harcourt), 2013.

[4] Cf. Bourgeault, *Wisdom Jesus, op. cit.*, pp. 14-21.

[5] Cf. Esther DeBoer, *Mary Magdalene: Beyond the Myth* (Trinity Press International), 1997, p. 115.

The Gospel of Judas: The Sarcastic Gospel

Bibliography

Barnstone, Willis, *The Restored New Testament: A New Translation with Commentary, Including the Gnostic Gospels Thomas, Mary, and Judas* (W.W. Norton & Company), 2009

Bourgeault, Cynthia, *The Wisdom Jesus: Transforming Heart and Mind – a New Perspective on Christ and His Message* (Shambhala), 2008

Bourgeault, Cynthia, "Gnosis and Gnosticism," on-line lecture, http://www.contemplative.org/pdfs/Gnosis_Gnosticism_CB_April_2010.pdf, last accessed May 3, 2014

DeBoer, Esther, *Mary Magdalene: Beyond the Myth* (Trinity Press International), 1997

DeConick, April D., "Gospel Truth," *The New York Times*, Op-Ed page, December 1, 2007, on-line at http://www.nytimes.com/2007/12/01/opinion/01deconink.html, last accessed May 3, 2014.

DeConick, April D., ed., *The Codex Judas Papers: Proceedings of the International Congress on the Tchacos Codex held at Rice University, Houston, Texas, March 13-16, 2008* (Brill), 2009

DeConick, April D., *The Thirteenth Apostle: What the Gospel of Judas Really Says* (Continuum), 2007, rev. ed. 2009

Ehrman, Bart D., *The Lost Gospel of Judas Iscariot: A New Look at Betrayer and Betrayed* (Oxford University Press), 2006

Jenott, Lance, *The Gospel of Judas: Coptic Text, Translation, and Historical Interpretation of the 'Betrayer's Gospel'* (Mohr Siebeck), 2011

Kasser, Rodolphe, and Gregor Wurst, *The Gospel of Judas, Critical Edition: Together with the Letter of Peter to Philip, James, and a Book of Allogenes from Codex Tchacos* (National Geographic), 2007

King, Karen L., *What Is Gnosticism?* (Belknap), 2003

Krosney, Herbert, Marvin Meyer, and Gregor Wurst, "Preliminary Report on New Fragments of Codex Tchacos" *Early Christianity* 1 (2010), pp. 282-294

Lambdin, Thomas O., *Introduction to Sahidic Coptic* (Mercer University Press), 1983

Layton, Bentley, *Coptic in 20 Lessons: Introduction to Sahidic Coptic With Exercises and Vocabularies* (Peeters), 2007

Leloup, Jean-Yves, *Judas and Jesus: Two Faces of a Single Revelation* (Inner Traditions), 2007

Mattison, Mark M., *The Gospel of Mary: A Fresh Translation and Holistic Approach* (CreateSpace Independent Publishing Platform), 2013

McDonald, Lee M., *The Formation of the Christian Biblical Canon* (Hendrickson Publishers), 1995

Meyer, Marvin, ed., *The Nag Hammadi Scriptures: The International Edition* (HarperOne), 2008

Miller, John W., *The Origins of the Bible: Rethinking Canon History* (Paulist Press), 1994

Pagels, Elaine and Karen L. King, *Reading Judas: The Gospel of Judas and the Shaping of Christianity* (Viking), 2007

Pappas, Stephanie, "Truth Behind Gospel of Judas Revealed in Ancient Inks," *LiveScience,* April 8, 2013, on-line at http://www.livescience.com/28506-gospel-judas-ink-authenticity.html, last accessed May 3, 2014.

Taussig, Hal, ed., *The New New Testament: A Bible for the 21st Century Combining Traditional and Newly Discovered Texts* (Houghton Mifflin Harcourt), 2013

Williams, Michael Allen, *Rethinking "Gnosticism": An Argument for Dismantling a Dubious Category* (Princeton University Press), 1996

Wright, N.T., *Judas and the Gospel of Jesus: Have We Missed the Truth about Christianity?* (Baker Books), 2006

Made in the USA
Columbia, SC
23 April 2023